★ **GREAT SPORTS TEAMS** ★

THE LOS ANGELES

BASKETBALL TEAM

William W. Lace

Enslow Publishers, Inc.

44 Fadem Road   PO Box 38
Box 699   Aldershot
Springfield, NJ 07081   Hants GU12 6BP
USA   UK

Library of Congress Cataloging-in-Publication Data

Lace, William W.
    The Los Angeles Lakers basketball team / William W. Lace.
       p. cm. — (Great Sports teams)
    Includes bibliographical references (p.) and index.
    Summary: Chronicles the history of the professional basketball franchise
that moved from Minneapolis to Los Angeles in 1960, discussing owners,
coaches, players, and the team's ten NBA Championships.
    ISBN 0-7660-1020-1
    1. Los Angeles Lakers (Basketball team)—History—Juvenile literature.
2. Minnesota Lakers (Basketball team)—History—Juvenile literature.
[1. Los Angeles Lakers (Basketball team)—History. 2. Minnesota Lakers
(Basketball team)—History. 3. Basketball—History.] I. Title. II. Series.
GV885.52.L67L33 1998
796.323'64'0979494—dc21   97-20074
                                           CIP
                                           AC

Printed in the United States of America

10 9 8 7 6 5 4 3 2 1

Illustration Credits: AP/Wide World Photos, pp. 4, 7, 8, 10, 13, 14, 16, 19, 20, 22, 25, 26, 28, 31, 32, 34, 37, 38.

Cover Illustration: AP/Wide World Photos.

CONTENTS

*K*areem Abdul-Jabbar attempts to block Julius Erving as he goes up for a basket in the 1980 NBA Finals.

A MAGIC MOMENT

The Los Angeles Lakers were in trouble. They led the Philadelphia 76ers, three games to two, in the 1980 National Basketball Association (NBA) Finals. They needed only one more victory to be the NBA champions, but Kareem Abdul-Jabbar—their team captain, leading scorer, and rebounder—was out with a sprained ankle.

With Abdul-Jabbar home in Los Angeles, Lakers Coach Paul Westhead had to decide who to start at center in his place at Philadelphia. He chose a twenty-year-old rookie named Earvin "Magic" Johnson.

"No problem, Paul," Johnson said when he heard the news. "I played some center in high school. It's beautiful to be in a situation like this."[1]

Playing to Win

Westhead didn't think it was so beautiful. He was just hoping Abdul-Jabbar's ankle would heal in time for a seventh game. In the locker room before the game, however, he was confident. "The last thing I said to the team before they went on the floor," he said later, "was that everyone expects an emotional game because we haven't got Kareem. I told them we didn't come here for courage. We came here to win."[2]

The Lakers had gone without winning a long time. They had been NBA champions five times in Minneapolis, Minnesota, but they had won only one title—in 1972—since moving to Los Angeles in 1960. Seven times they had made the finals. Seven times they had lost—six times to the Boston Celtics. People were saying that they were chokers; that they were the "Fakers," not the Lakers.

Looking for Kareem

The 76ers almost didn't believe it when the six-foot nine-inch Johnson walked to center court to jump against Philadelphia's seven-foot one-inch Caldwell Jones. Their coach, Billy Cunningham, had said, "I'll believe [Abdul-Jabbar's] not coming when the game ends and I haven't seen him."[3]

Cunningham never saw Abdul-Jabbar that night, but he saw more of Magic Johnson than he wanted. Johnson didn't win the tip, but he did everything else. Early in the game he took a pass at the top of the free-throw lane, wheeled, and drove toward the basket. "I wanted to dunk it, like Kareem," he said after the game, "but I saw [Daryl] Dawkins coming and I thought, well, I better change it to something a little more . . . *magical*."[4]

*M*agic Johnson sails for a layup. One of the greatest point guards of all-time, Johnson was forced to play center in the 1980 NBA Finals.

Magic Johnson took special delight in the Lakers 1980 championship. The twenty-year-old rookie was named the Lakers' Most Valuable Player of the 1980 NBA Finals.

Johnson sailed into the air, hung there for an unbelievably long moment, pumped twice, and laid the ball in the basket over the six-foot eleven-inch Dawkins, drawing a foul in the process.

Putting It Away

The game was tied at the half, but the Lakers—led by Jamaal Wilkes—reeled off 14 straight points to open the second half. Wilkes scored 16 of his 37 points in the third quarter.

The 76ers fought back and trailed by only two points, 103-101, with 5:12 left in the game. After a Lakers' timeout, Johnson tipped in a rebound, Wilkes hit a layup and a free throw, and Los Angeles won, going away with a 123-107 victory. Johnson scored 9 points in the game's final 2:22.

Johnson finished the night with 42 points, 15 rebounds, and 7 assists. He was named Most Valuable Player (MVP) of the series. "The big difference was Magic," said Westhead, "He was like Houdini out there."[5]

Dancin' in L.A.

In the locker room, an exhausted Johnson was interviewed on television. He looked into the camera and spoke to Abdul-Jabbar. "We know you're hurtin' Big Fella, but we want you to get up and do a little dancin' tonight." Back in Los Angeles, Abdul-Jabbar got out of bed and did "a little hippity-hop step," sore ankle and all.[6]

Lakers owner Jerry Buss, his hair soaked with champagne, accepted the championship trophy from NBA Commissioner Larry O'Brien. He hugged the trophy and said, "You don't know how long I've waited for this moment."[7]

All the Lakers fans knew how he felt. After so many disappointments, they once again had a champion.

Professional basketball grew up in the Midwest. In this 1942 game, the Oshkosh Stars defeated the Detroit Eagles to win the National Pro Basketball Championship.

INSTANT DYNASTY

In the fall of 1946, sportswriter Sid Hartman thought that Minneapolis was ready for professional basketball. He talked a friend, businessman Ben Berger, into sponsoring a game there. They wanted to see if there was any interest among fans.

Sure enough, more than 5,500 fans packed Minneapolis Auditorium to see two National Basketball League (NBL) teams—Oshkosh and Sheboygan. Berger was convinced. In July 1947 he, Hartman, and promoter Morris Chalfen bought the Detroit Gems of the National Basketball League for $15,000. Since Minnesota was known as "the Land of Ten Thousand Lakes," they decided to call their team the Lakers.

Professional basketball had been around since 1898, only seven years after the game was invented. The National Basketball League had been formed in 1937.

Three Good Deals

The Lakers' owners had to move fast. They had no coach and no players, and the season was only three months away. They solved the coaching problem first, hiring John Kundla away from St. Thomas College in nearby St. Paul. The Lakers then made two moves that would make the team an instant success. The signings of Jim Pollard, a former star at Stanford University, and six-foot ten-inch George Mikan.

Mikan had been a three-time All-American at DePaul University in Chicago. When the 1947 season began, he was a member of the Chicago Gears of the Professional Basketball League of America. That league went out of business shortly after the season started, however, and Mikan signed with the Lakers.

The Lakers promptly won the 1948 NBL championship. The next year, the team moved to the Basketball Association of America (BAA) and won that league's title too. In 1949 the NBL and the BAA merged to form the National Basketball Association (NBA). With Mikan averaging 27.4 points a game, the Lakers became the first NBA champions in 1949–50.

The Lakers had won three championships in three leagues in their first three years. Led by Mikan, Pollard, Vern Mikkelsen, and Slater Martin, they would win the NBA title three out of the next four years as well.

Hard Times

After Mikan retired in 1954, the Lakers had six straight losing seasons. The team almost moved to St. Louis, Missouri, in 1957. A group of investors, led by

*M*inneapolis Lakers coach John Kundla chats with Elgin Baylor, who signed with the Lakers in 1958. Kundla led the Lakers to five NBA championships in six years.

Bob Short, bought the team from the original owners and kept it in Minneapolis.

The losing streak continued. The big crowds shrank. In 1957 Short thought about moving the team. He said, "At our present artistic and financial pace, we couldn't operate here next season"[1]

The Lakers' record and attendance improved over the next two years, thanks to the exciting play of newcomer Elgin Baylor. "If he had turned me down," Short said of his negotiations with Baylor, "I would have been out of business."[2]

Heading West

The improvement in attendance was not enough. On April 28, 1960, Short announced that the team would

*T*he Lakers traded three players to the Philadelphia 76ers for star center Wilt Chamberlain in 1968.

move to Los Angeles the next season. They would continue to be called the Lakers, even though Los Angeles has almost no lakes. "I couldn't call them the Oceaneers," said Short.[3]

At first the Lakers were not a Hollywood hit. Average attendance was only 5,045 in 1960–61. Four years later, however, the average was more than 10,000.

In 1965, Short sold the team to Jack Kent Cooke. Cooke wanted to bring new life to the Lakers. He built his own arena, the Forum. He changed the team colors to purple and gold. He spent huge amounts of money on players, including a trade for center Wilt Chamberlain, who led the Lakers to an NBA title in 1972.

A New Owner

In 1979 Cooke decided to leave California. He traded the Lakers, the Forum, and his Los Angeles Kings hockey team to real estate developer Jerry Buss for properties in the East. The deal was worth almost $70 million.

Buss wanted Lakers games to be the most exciting events in Los Angeles. He hired a band to replace the traditional organist. He introduced the Laker Girls dance team. All this was combined with a fast-paced Lakers' offense. "Showtime," as it came to be called, had arrived.

*G*eorge Mikan was the first great star of the National Basketball Association. He led the Minneapolis Lakers to five NBA championships in the early days of the NBA.

KINGS OF THE COURT

n their half-century of basketball, the Lakers have had many outstanding players. From George Mikan in 1947 Minneapolis to Shaquille O'Neal in 1997 Los Angeles, some of the greatest names in the game have thrilled generations of fans.

George Mikan

For years the Lakers' offense was simple. They waited until George Mikan was in position under the opponents' basket and got him the ball. Once there, he was almost unstoppable. Mikan led the Lakers in scoring seven straight seasons and led the league three times.

"I've seen and coached many great players," said Bud Grant, a Lakers teammate and later a National Football League coach. "I'd have to say George was the greatest competitor I've seen or been around in any sport."[1]

Elgin Baylor

"Elgin Baylor," said one NBA team executive, "was the Michael Jordan of his day. That's the only guy you could compare him to."[2] Like Jordan, Baylor's specialty was seeming to float through the air forever and then slamming the ball through the basket.

In his fourteen seasons, Baylor averaged 27.4 points per game—the best in Lakers' history. His best night ever came on November 15, 1960, when he scored a Lakers record 71 points in New York. He also holds the team scoring record for a playoff game, 61 points against Boston in 1962.

Jerry West

When quiet, shy Jerry West arrived in Los Angeles from West Virginia, Baylor nicknamed him "Zeke from Cabin Creek." On the court, however, he was strictly big-time. "When you begin talking about the all-around great players of basketball, a pretty good starting point is Jerry West," said Red Auerbach of the Boston Celtics.[3]

West could score from anywhere on the court. In the fifth game of the 1970 NBA Finals, the New York Knicks scored, with three seconds left, to go ahead by two points. West took the inbounds pass, dribbled three times, and launched a shot that soared sixty-three feet and into the basket, forcing overtime.

West averaged 29.1 points in playoff games, second in NBA history only to Michael Jordan.

The Los Angeles Lakers Basketball Team

*J*erry West continued the great trendsetting tradition of the Los Angeles Lakers. His image is used on the NBA's logo.

Shaquille O'Neal is one of the great young stars of the NBA. Los Angeles fans hope he can lead their team back to its championship-winning ways.

Kareem Abdul-Jabbar

With 8:53 left in a game on April 5, 1984, Kareem Abdul-Jabbar hit a basket. It gave him a career point total of 31,420, breaking Chamberlain's record.

The shot was Abdul-Jabbar's famous "sky hook," which according to coach Pat Riley was "the most deadly and unstoppable offensive weapon in any sport."[4]

Before he changed his name from Lew Alcindor, Abdul-Jabbar led his college team, UCLA, to three straight National Collegiate Athletic Association (NCAA) championships and led the Milwaukee Bucks to an NBA title. Traded to the Lakers in 1975, he went on to set NBA career records for games played (1,560), total points (38,387), and blocked shots (3,189).

The Los Angeles Lakers Basketball Team

Former Boston center Bill Russell said, "I think Kareem Abdul-Jabbar will be remembered as the greatest center ever."[5]

Earvin "Magic" Johnson

Before the 1979–80 season, the Lakers were a good team. That season they became a great team. "The dramatic difference was Magic," said Abdul-Jabbar. "It was like night and day as far as what we were capable of doing."[6]

Combining the size of a forward (six-foot nine-inches) with the quickness of a guard, Johnson excelled at all parts of the game. He took more pride in passing the ball than in anything else, and once held the NBA record for career assists with 10,141. He once said, "If I make a great pass to Michael Cooper and he goes in for a dunk, it still gets me high."[7]

Shaquille O'Neal

The Lakers continued their tradition of having great centers by signing Shaquille O'Neal in 1996.

O'Neal has been a dominating force ever since coming into the league. In his four seasons with the Orlando Magic, he averaged 27.2 points and 12.5 rebounds a game. With O'Neal at center, the Lakers hope to improve their defense, too. "He creates a lot of problems for other teams defensively with his offense and he's a force on defense," said NBC commentator Peter Vecsey. "You have to earn your points when you go against Shaq."[8]

*J*ack Kent Cooke stands in front of The Forum, the arena he built for Southern California's first NBA team.

THE LEADERSHIP

The Lakers franchise has won ten NBA championships, more than any other team except Boston. Four names stand out in the Lakers' long history of successful leadership—Jack Kent Cooke, Bill Sharman, Pat Riley, and Jerry Buss.

Jack Kent Cooke

In 1965 Jack Kent Cooke decided he wanted the Lakers. Although Bob Short did not especially want to sell the team, he couldn't turn down what was then a phenomenal offer of $5,175,000.

Cooke could afford it. A native of Canada, he had made a fortune in publishing and cable television. "I was rather well off and could indulge myself," he said of his purchase.[1]

Cooke set out to make the Lakers the most glamorous team in the NBA. He built the Forum and ordered his staff always to refer to it as the "Fabulous"

Forum. While every other NBA team wore white uniforms at home, Cooke's Lakers wore gold.

He was a tough boss but a fair one. "No one ever had any misunderstanding about what I wanted done," he said. "In that respect I was easy to work for."[2]

Bill Sharman

Bill Sharman was no stranger to the Lakers when he became coach in 1971. They had seen more than enough of him when he played on four NBA Championship teams with the Boston Celtics.

Sharman was the first NBA coach to have his team work out almost every day. He created the "shoot-around," a brief workout on game days. His work habits paid off as the Lakers won the NBA Championship in his first year as coach.

Sharman was a fierce competitor, both as a player and as a coach. "It didn't matter if it was basketball or ping-pong," he said. "I always liked to finish first. For some reason, I hated to get beat at anything."[3]

Sharman drove himself so hard screaming at his players that he strained his vocal cords and was eventually unable to coach. He moved to the front office, and as general manager and then president, guided the Lakers to five more titles.

Pat Riley

Even after his Lakers won the NBA Championship in 1982, some people didn't give Pat Riley either credit or respect. Anyone, they said, could win a title with

*I*n 1971, Cook (center) hired two former Celtics K.C. Jones (left) and Bill Sharman (right) to coach the Lakers. A year later, the Lakers won their first NBA championship since 1954.

Kareem Abdul-Jabbar and Magic Johnson on his team. "What some people don't realize," said Riley, "is that I *did* pay my dues. I was in this game for 20 years—studying and observing, filing things away."[4]

In 1967 Riley was the first-round draft choice (seventh overall) of the San Diego Rockets. In 1971 he was traded to the Lakers. He spent most of his five seasons in Los Angeles as a backup, averaging about 10 points a game.

In 1979 he became Paul Westhead's assistant. When Westhead was fired early in the 1981–82 season, Riley became head coach. He became the most successful coach in Lakers' history, winning four championships and more than 72 percent of his games.

*W*hile Pat Riley's slicked-back hair made him a nationally recognized figure, it was his coaching talent that brought the Lakers four NBA championships in the 1980s.

Jerry Buss

Jerry Buss has come a long way. He owns the Lakers and a stable of race horses. Not bad for a guy who dug ditches as a teenager and once dropped out of high school.

Buss returned to school and eventually earned a Ph.D. in chemistry at the University of Southern California. He worked briefly in the aerospace industry. In 1958 he and fellow scientist Frank Mariani started a small real estate business. Seven years later, at the age of thirty-four, he was a millionaire.

His first venture in sports was ownership of a pro tennis team in 1972. It lost money, but, as Buss said, "This is going to be my education in sports."[5]

In wasn't until 1979, when he bought the Lakers and Kings from Cooke, that Buss's dream of owning a major sports team came true. In his first ten years as the Lakers' owner, he put the team at the top of the NBA, winning five championships. In 1990 the Associated Press named Buss's Lakers the Professional Sports Franchise of the Decade.

*G*eorge Mikan (#99), jumps high to slap the ball to Jim Pollard (#17) in the 1949 BAA (Basketball Association of America) playoffs. The Lakers won the series, 4-2.

SWEET MEMORIES

The Lakers have had many outstanding seasons. They have reached the NBA Finals twenty-four times and won eleven championships. Perhaps the three top seasons in Lakers' history are 1949–50, when they became the NBA's first champions; 1971–72, when they won their first title in Los Angeles; and 1984–85, when they finally beat the Boston Celtics.

Start of a Dynasty

The National Basketball Association was formed in 1949, when teams from both the Basketball Association of America and National Basketball League merged. It made little difference, since the name of the champion was the same—the Lakers.

Minneapolis had already won back-to-back titles in both the NBL and the BAA. The Lakers, with Mikan at center and Pollard at forward, were already a great team. They got even better before the 1949–50 season by adding guard Slater Martin of Texas and Vern Mikkelsen of Hamline.

At first, Mikkelsen was Mikan's backup at center. Then, Coach John Kundla positioned Mikkelsen and Mikan close to the basket, making Mikkelsen basketball's first power forward. "My function wasn't to score," Mikkelsen said. "It was mainly to rebound and play defense."[1]

Behind the passing of Martin and the shooting and rebounding of what was then the tallest front line in the league, the Lakers stormed to a 51-17 regular season record. They swept playoff series with Chicago; Fort Wayne; and Anderson, Indiana, to meet the Syracuse Nationals in the Finals.

After the Lakers forged a 3-2 lead, the Nationals tried to tie the series in Game 6 by playing as rough as possible. It didn't do them any good. In a game marred by several fights and ejections, the Lakers won 110-95 for the first-ever NBA Championship.

California Dreamin'

In their first ten years in Los Angeles, the Lakers went to the NBA Finals seven times—and lost all seven. Things finally changed in 1971–72.

On November 5 the Lakers beat Baltimore and went on to win thirty-two more games in a row. They finally lost on January 9 to Kareem Abdul-Jabbar and the Milwaukee Bucks. The thirty-three-game winning streak is still an NBA record. Wilt Chamberlain wasn't

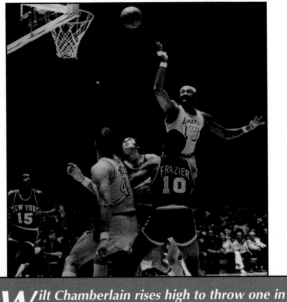

Wilt Chamberlain rises high to throw one in over the heads of the Knicks' Walt Frazier, Jerry Lucas, and Earl Monroe (#15). The Lakers Jerry West (#4) looks on.

all that impressed. "I played for the Harlem Globetrotters," he said, "and we won 445 in a row."[2]

The Lakers finished the regular season 69-13, the highest winning percentage ever. They scored more than 100 points in 81 of their 82 games. West and Gail Goodrich both averaged more than 25 points a game. Chamberlain yanked down 19.2 rebounds a game.

In the playoffs the Lakers swept the Chicago Bulls, then eliminated Abdul-Jabbar's Bucks in six games. In the Finals against New York, the Knicks won the first game, but that was all. The Lakers reeled off four straight victories. In the final game Chamberlain, his injured wrist heavily taped, scored 24 points and grabbed 29 rebounds.

James Worthy was an important part of the Lakers 1980s championship teams. He was awarded the 1988 NBA Finals MVP for his part in defeating the Boston Celtics.

By the mid-1980s the Lakers had accomplished just about every achievement in pro basketball except for one. They had never beaten Boston in the playoffs, falling to the Celtics eight times.

When the 1985 NBA Finals began in Boston, it appeared the Lakers' woes would continue. In Game 1 they were crushed, 148-114, in what sports writers called the "Memorial Day Massacre."

The Lakers changed their strategy. They would still play a fast-paced game, but they would also try to be as physical as the Celtics. "It's like the bully on the block who keeps taking your lunch money every day," said Lakers Assistant Coach Dave Wohl. "Finally you get tired of it, and you whack him."[3]

That's exactly what the Lakers did. They beat Boston, 109-102 and 136-111, in Games 2 and 3. The Celtics won by two points in Game 4, but Los Angeles took Game 5 to move within one victory of the title.

Game 6 was at the Boston Garden. No team had ever defeated Boston on the Celtics' home court to win an NBA championship. The Lakers, however, were unstoppable. Kareem Abdul-Jabbar got 29 points. James Worthy added 28. Magic Johnson had a triple-double—14 points, 14 assists, and 10 rebounds. The Lakers had finally broken the Boston jinx, 111-100.

Team owner Jerry Buss took a piece of paper from his pocket. On it he wrote, "The Lakers have never beaten the Celtics."[4] He looked at it for a moment, then happily marked through the word never.

*T*he Los Angeles Lakers hope that star center Shaquille O'Neal can lead them back to the NBA championship.

SHAQ AND BEYOND

As the 1996–97 season rolled around, the Los Angeles Lakers had been absent from the NBA throne room for eight seasons—a long dry spell for this franchise. In three of their last six seasons, they had been bounced from the playoffs in the first round. In 1994 they did not even make the playoffs. It was only the fourth time in history that they weren't around for the postseason.

Gone was Abdul-Jabbar, who had retired in 1989. Gone was Magic Johnson, who came out of retirement briefly in 1995–96 and then re-retired. Owner Jerry Buss and Executive Vice President Jerry West knew they had to make some major moves if the Lakers were again to be a championship contender.

The Lakers had been in the same position before. Both times they went out and got a dominating center—Chamberlain in 1968 and Abdul-Jabbar in 1975. The strategy had worked twice. Why not try it again?

Signing O'Neal

In the summer of 1996 the Lakers signed Shaquille O'Neal. O'Neal, a seven-foot one-inch giant, had led the NBA in scoring in 1994–95 and had been near the league lead in rebounding every year.

O'Neal also is one of the most animated players in the NBA and was an instant favorite with the Lakers' crowds. "This guy's going to be the biggest star in L.A.," said West.[1]

Lakers Coach Del Harris thinks O'Neal is a valuable addition—not only in talent, but also in personality.

"What I appreciate about him, as much as anything, is that I think he is a dedicated basketball player," Harris said. "He wants to improve and he wants to win games and yet he's got such a lighthearted spirit about him from time to time that can break up a pressure situation. I believe that over the course of 82 games, that kind of personality is going to wear very well with our team and in general."[2]

More Lakers' Talent

The Lakers' talent does not stop with O'Neal. Guard Nick Van Exel has become one of the league's best three-point shooters. Forward Elden Campbell continues to improve. He blocked more shots (212) in 1995–96 than any Lakers player in fifteen seasons.

The Lakers also have one of the NBA's most exciting young players in Kobe Bryant. Bryant was barely eighteen years old when he played his first Lakers' game. He came to the pros straight out of high school.

In a controversial move, the Lakers made a draft-day trade with the Charlotte Hornets to obtain Kobe Bryant prior to the 1996 season.

*E*ddie Jones shows off the MVP he was awarded for his performance in the 1995 Rookie All-Star Game. Jones was the Lakers #1 draft pick in 1994.

"He [Bryant] was, by far, the most skilled player we have ever worked out," said West.[3]

The outlook at guard is also brightened by Eddie Jones. Jones was the Lakers' No. 1 draft choice in 1994. He has led the team in steals in each of his two seasons. He was selected on the first team of the NBA's All-Rookie team.

Mid-Season Trade

With O'Neal at center, the Lakers improved at once in 1996–97. Buss and West, however, were not satisfied. In January 1997 they pulled off a huge trade with

Phoenix, swapping Cedric Ceballos and Rumeal Robinson for the Suns' Robert Horry and Joe Kleine. The six-foot ten-inch Horry is a solid defender and a good outside shooter for his size.

The 1996–97 Lakers finished second in the Pacific Division despite Shaquille O'Neal missing two months of action due to an injury. O'Neal returned in time for the start of the playoffs, but the Lakers found limited success. After defeating the Portland Trailblazers in the first round, Los Angeles fell to Utah in the Conference Semifinals in five games. However, with their good young team the Lakers are sure to be a force to be reckoned with in 1997–98.

The Lakers' future, however, will be built on O'Neal. His scoring and rebounding ability is unquestioned. He must, however, improve his free-throw shooting percentage. He made only 48.7 percent in 1995–96, one of the worst in the NBA.

Some people have also questioned O'Neal's desire. They have said he is too interested in other things, like making movies and recording rap music, to become a great player. O'Neal says that's not the case. He wants a championship.

"That's where I want to go," he wrote. "No, that's where I have to go. I know that all the commercials, all the press stories won't mean anything unless I get a championship."[4]

STATISTICS

Team Record

The Lakers History

YEARS	LOCATION	W	L	PCT	CHAMPIONSHIPS
1947–48— 1949–50	Minneapolis	138	50	.734	1948*, 1949, 1950
1950–51— 1959–60	Minneapolis	362	349	.509	1952, 1953, 1954
1960–61— 1969–70	Los Angeles	468	338	.581	None
1970–71— 1979–80	Los Angeles	499	321	.609	1972, 1980
1980–81— 1989–90	Los Angeles	594	226	.724	1982, 1985, 1987, 1988
1990–91— 1996–97	Los Angeles	330	244	.575	None

*National Basketball League (NBL) Champions

The Lakers Today

SEASON	SEASON RECORD	PLAYOFF RECORD	COACH	DIVISION FINISH
1990–91	58-24	12-7	Mike Dunleavy	2nd
1991–92	43-39	1-3	Mike Dunleavy	6th
1992–93	39-43	2-3	Randy Pfund	5th
1993–94	33-49	—	Randy Pfund Bill Bertka Earvin Johnson	5th
1994–95	48-34	5-5	Del Harris	3rd
1995–96	53-29	1-3	Del Harris	2nd
1996–97	56-26	4-5	Del Harris	2nd

Total History

SEASON RECORD	PLAYOFF RECORD	NBA CHAMPIONSHIPS
2,391-1,528	313-213	11

Coaching Records

COACH	YEARS COACHED	RECORD	CHAMPIONSHIPS
John Kundla	1947–59	465-319	Division Champions, 1950–51, NBL Champions, 1947–48 BAA Champions, 1948–49 NBA Champions, 1949–50, 1951–52, 1952–53, 1953–54
Herman Schaefer	1950–51	1-0	None
George Mikan	1957–58	9-30	None
John Castellani	1959–60	11-25	None
Jim Pollard	1959–60	14-25	None
Fred Schaus	1960–67	315-245	Division Champions, 1961–62, 1962–63, 1964–65, 1965–66
Bill Van Breda Kolff	1967–69	107-57	Division Champions, 1968–69
Joe Mullaney	1969–71	94-70	Division Champions, 1970–71
Bill Sharman	1971–76	246-164	Division Champions, 1972–73, 1973–74 NBA Champions, 1971–72
Jerry West	1976–79	145-101	Division Champions, 1976–77
Jack McKinney	1979	9-4	None
Paul Westhead	1979–81	112-50	NBA Champions, 1979–80
Pat Riley	1981–90	533-194	Division Champions, 1982–83, 1983–84, 1985–86, 1988–89, 1989–90 NBA Champions, 1981–82, 1984–85, 1986–87, 1987–88
Mike Dunleavy	1990–92	101-63	None
Randy Pfund	1992–94	66-80	None
Bill Bertka	1994	1-1	None
Earvin Johnson	1994	5-11	None
Del Harris	1994–	157-89	None

Ten Great Lakers

		CAREER STATISTICS							
PLAYER	SEA	YRS	G	REB	AST	BLK	STL	PTS	AVG
Kareem Abdul-Jabbar	1975–89	20	1,560	17,440	5,660	3,189	1,160	38,387	24.6
Elgin Baylor	1958–72	14	846	11,463	3,650	*	*	23,149	27.4
Wilt Chamberlain	1968–73	14	1,045	23,924	4,643	*	*	31,419	30.1
Gail Goodrich	1965–68, 1970–76	14	1,031	3,279	4,805	72*	545*	19,181	18.6
Earvin "Magic" Johnson	1979–91, 1995–96	13	906	6,559	10,141	688	1,503	17,707	19.5
George Mikan**	1947–54, 1955–56	9	439	4,167*	1,245*	*	*	10,156	23.1
Shaquille O'Neal	1996–97	5	346	4,331	875	971	289	9,355	27.0
Byron Scott	1984–93, 1996–97	14	1,073	2,987	2,729	276	1,224	15,097	14.1
Jerry West	1960–74	14	932	5,376	6,238	23*	81*	25,192	27.0
James Worthy	1982–94	12	926	4,708	2,791	624	1,041	16,320	17.6

* Statistics are incomplete for some players in some categories. The NBA did not keep statistics on rebounds until 1950–51 and on steals and blocked shots until 1973–74.

** Includes statistics prior to formation of NBA.

SEA=Seasons with Lakers
YRS=Years in the NBA
G=Games
REB=Rebounds
AST=Assists

BLK=Blocks
STL=Steals
PTS=Total Points
AVG=Scoring Average

The Los Angeles Lakers Basketball Team

CHAPTER NOTES

Chapter 1

1. Scott Ostler and Steve Springer, *Winnin' Times* (New York: Macmillan Publishing Company, 1986), p. 6.

2. The Associated Press, "Lakers Shock Sixers," *Houston Post,* May 16, 1980, p. 1C.

3. John Papanek, "Arms and the Man," *Sports Illustrated,* May 26, 1980, p. 20.

4. Ibid., p. 21.

5. Associated Press, p. 1C.

6. Papanek, p. 23.

7. Ostler and Springer, p. 13.

Chapter 2

1. Stew Thornley, *The History of the Lakers* (Minneapolis, Minn.: Nodin Press, 1989), p. 64.

2. Ibid., p. 65.

3. Scott Ostler and Steve Springer, *Winnin' Times* (New York: Macmillan Publishing Company, 1986), p. 52.

Chapter 3

1. Joseph Hession, *Lakers: Collector's Edition* (San Francisco: Foghorn Press, 1994), p. 37.

2. Ibid., p. 47.

3. *Lincoln Library of Sports Champions* (Columbus, Oh.: Frontier Press Company, 1989), vol. 19, p. 8.

4. Pat Riley, *Show Time: Inside the Lakers' Breakthrough Season* (New York: Warner Books, 1988), p. 49.

5. John Devaney, *The Story of Basketball* (New York: Random House, 1976), p. 207.

6. Scott Ostler and Steve Springer, *Winnin' Times* (New York: Macmillan Publishing Company, 1986), p. 52.

7. Steve Delsohn, *Showtime* (Chicago: Contemporary Books, Inc., 1985), p. 63.

8. Michael J. Sullivan, *Sports Great Shaquille O'Neal* (Springfield, N.J.: Enslow Publishers, Inc., 1995), p. 37.

Chapter 4

1. Scott Ostler and Steve Springer, *Winnin' Times* (New York: Macmillan Publishing Company, 1986), p. 57.

2. Ibid., p. 58.

3. Joseph Hession, *Lakers: Collector's Edition* (San Francisco: Foghorn Press, 1994), p. 97.

4. Steve Delsohn, *Showtime* (Chicago: Contemporary Books, Inc., 1985), p. 118.

5. Ostler and Springer, p. 83.

Chapter 5

1. Stew Thornley, *The History of the Lakers* (Minneapolis, Minn.: Nodin Press, 1989), p. 28.

2. Joseph Hession, *Lakers: Collector's Edition* (San Francisco: Foghorn Press, 1994), p. 76.

3. Alexander Wolff, "The 'Movie Stars' Changed Their Act," *Sports Illustrated,* June 3, 1985, p. 36.

4. Scott Ostler and Steve Springer, *Winnin' Times* (New York: Macmillan Publishing Company, 1986), p. 287.

Chapter 6

1. Barry Rubinstein, "Have Fun, Drink Pepsi, Wear Reeboks," *Athlon Sports Pro Basketball* (Nashville, Tenn.: Athlon Sports Communications, 1996), p. 22.

2. "Lakers Looking Good: Q-A with Del Harris," Los Angeles Lakers Home Page, NBA Properties, Inc., January 11, 1997.

3. *Los Angeles Lakers 1996–97 Media Guide* (Los Angeles: The Los Angeles Lakers, 1996), p. 26.

4. Shaquille O'Neal, *Shaq Attaq* (New York: Hyperion, 1995), p. 202.

GLOSSARY

center—The player on a basketball team whose position is between the two forwards and closest to the basket. The center is usually the tallest player on the team.

draft—The selection, in rotating order, of college players each year by NBA teams. The teams with the worst records generally get to choose first.

forward—The players on a basketball team whose positions are on either side of the center along the end of the court. Forwards are usually among the taller players.

free throw—A shot awarded a player who is fouled by an opponent. The free throw is shot from a distance of fifteen feet and counts for one point.

guard—The players on a basketball team whose positions are more toward the midcourt line than the two forwards and the center. Guards are usually the shortest players on the team but are the best ball-handlers.

general manager—The official in charge of building the team by getting players either through the draft or by trades. The general manager is in charge of those aspects of the team not overseen by the coaching staff.

lottery—The system in the player draft where those teams not making the playoffs draw to determine the drafting order. The lottery was created to prevent teams from deliberately losing games to get the number one draft choice.

playoffs—The scheduling system that matches the NBA teams with the best records each year in a series of games to determine the champion.

point guard—The player on a basketball team who normally is the best ball-handler and whose job it is to bring the ball up the court and run the offense.

power forward—The forward who is usually taller and more physical than the other forward. The power forward's primary job often is to rebound.

rebound—The retrieving of a ball after a missed shot.

small forward—The forward who is mostly responsible for scoring. The small forward is usually shorter and not as good a rebounder as the power forward.

three-pointer—A shot from more than twenty-one feet from the basket that counts for three points if it is made.

 FURTHER READING

Anderson, Dave. *The Story of Basketball.* New York: William Morrow and Company Inc., 1988.

Bennett, Frank. *The Illustrated Rules of Basketball.* Nashville, Tenn.: Ideals Children's Books, 1994.

Cobourn, R. Thomas. *Kareem Abdul-Jabbar.* New York: Chelsea House Publishers, 1995.

Gutman, Bill. *The Kid's World Almanac of Basketball.* Mahwah, N.J.: Funk & Wagnalls Corp., 1995.

Haskins, James. *Sports Great Magic Johnson, Revised and Expanded.* Springfield, N.J.: Enslow Publishers, Inc., 1992.

Knapp, Ron. *Top 10 Basketball Centers.* Springfield, N.J.: Enslow Publishers, Inc., 1994.

Macnow, Glen. *Shaquille O'Neal: Star Center.* Springfield, N.J.: Enslow Publishers, Inc., 1996.

Mullin, Chris. *The Young Basketball Player.* New York: The Dorling Kindersley Publishing Company, 1995.

Norman, Jack. *Wilt Chamberlain: A Winner.* Chicago: Children's Press, 1973.

Sullivan, Michael J. *Sports Great Shaquille O'Neal.* Springfield, N.J.: Enslow Publishers, Inc., 1995.

INDEX

WHERE TO WRITE

Los Angeles Lakers
Post Office Box 10
Inglewood, CA
90306-2227

WEBSITE

http://www.nba.com/lakers